The Three Terrific Tweets

by

William Bootle

Grosvenor House
Publishing Limited

The right of William Bootle to be identified as the author of this
work has been asserted in accordance with Section 78
of the Copyright, Designs and Patents Act 1988

The book cover is copyright to William Bootle

This book is published by
Grosvenor House Publishing Ltd
Link House
140 The Broadway, Tolworth, Surrey, KT6 7HT.
www.grosvenorhousepublishing.co.uk

This book is a work of fiction. Any resemblance to
people or events, past or present, is purely coincidental.

A CIP record for this book
is available from the British Library

ISBN 978-1-83615-156-2

This book
belongs to

_____

_____

Message from author

My name is William Bootle, I was born in England in 2011. I wrote this book to share with the world the wonder of my pet chickens. This book originally started as a poem which I wrote over a year ago about how my chickens acted and behaved back then. From when the draft of this poem was written and the release of this book my pets attitudes and behaviour have changed drastically and I hope to write many more books in the future on how much of a change it's been since the original poem and also I would love to write books on other subjects as well.

The three terrific tweets

My chickens, oh how I adore them so,

Three wonderful souls,
let me let you know.

Izzy, Fluffy, Cindy each with their own tale,

I

C

F

Gather 'round listen close, let their stories unveil.

First there's Cindy, let's talk about her now,

Her first name is Cinderella,
brother's choice somehow.

Cuddles are her delight, it's absolutely true,

A Rhode Island red,
cleaning her poo,
not my favourite thing to do.

4

Unlike others, she's not shy, that's for sure,

Survival skills, she's got them strong and secure .

5

A hero, brightening my gloomy days,

In my heart, her love forever stay.

6

Cindy, a chicken with
feathers of gold,

Muscular calves, oh so bold.

She has a beak so shiny,

And her talons
are ever so tiny.

9

Cindy's heart is so big and bright,

Making sure we're
always alright.

Now let's talk about Fluffy, the creepy one.

With her gaze upon me, not all fun.

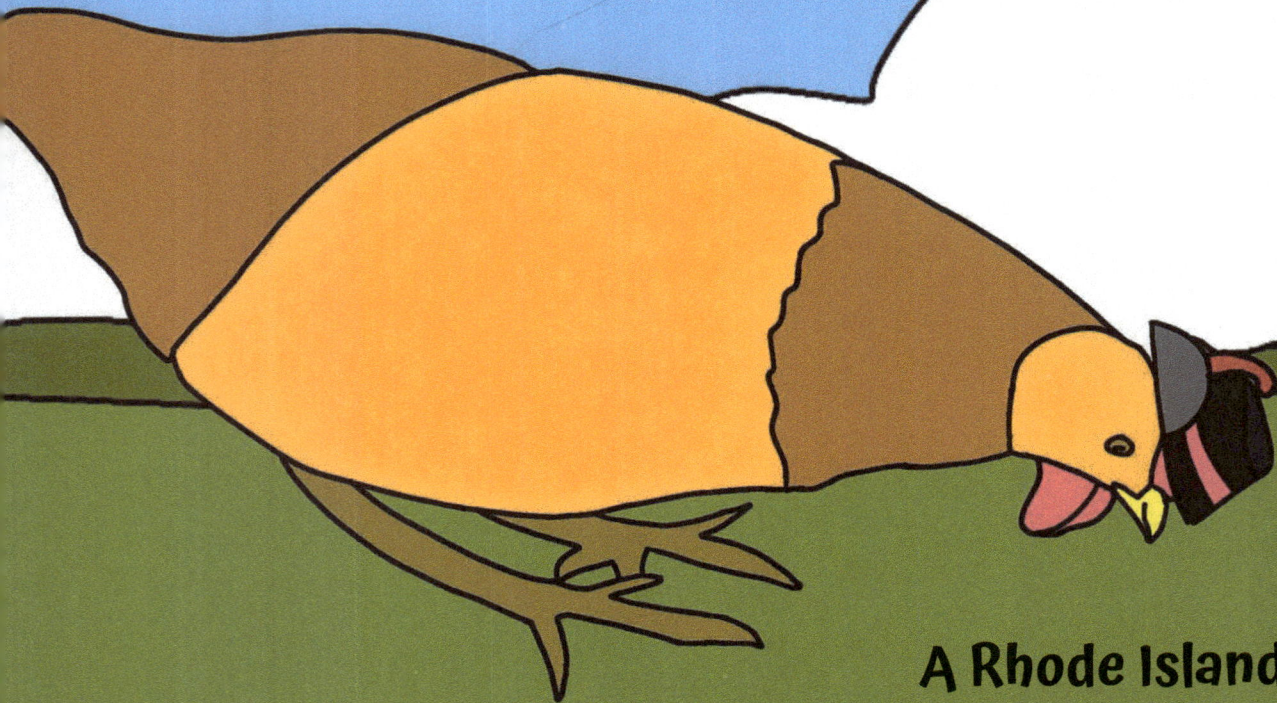

Same breed as super Cindy, you see,

A Rhode Island Red, needy as can be.

She reminds me of Aphmau, a cockerel we had before,

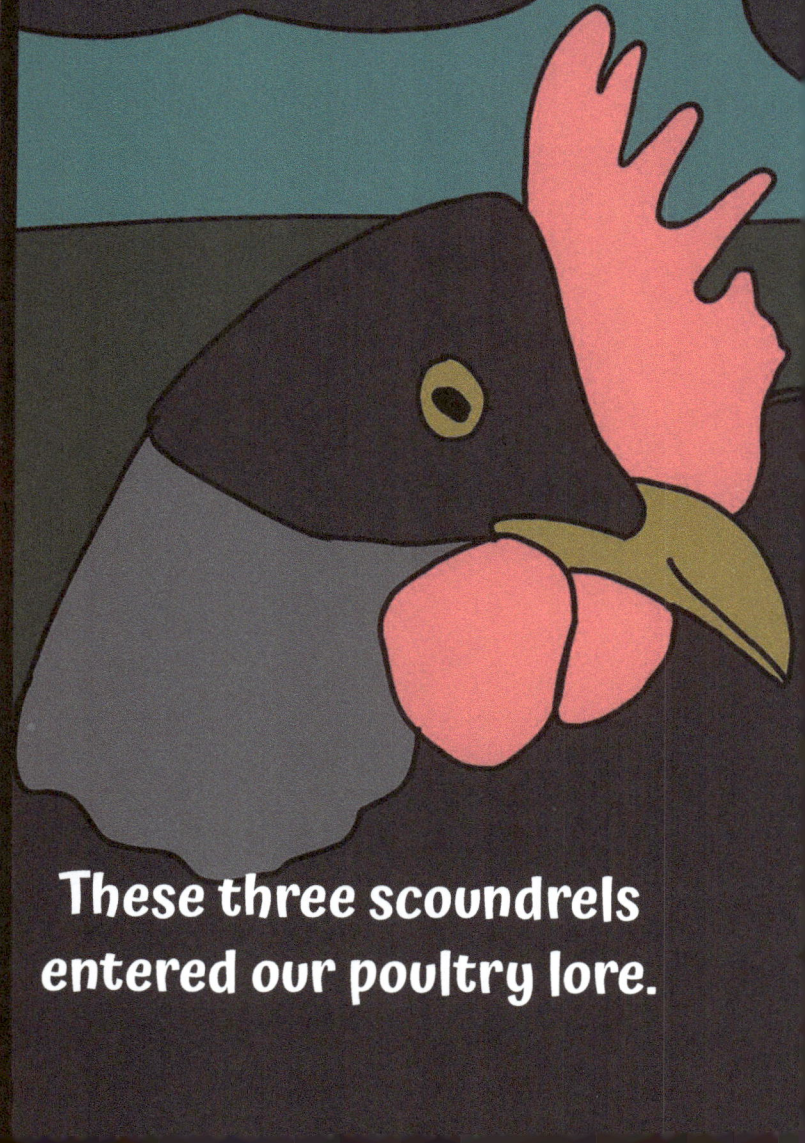

These three scoundrels entered our poultry lore.

14

When she was younger,
we thought she'd lead,

Leader (1st)

2nd

3rd

But now she'd content following the feed.

Her look upon others
makes her known,

But when I look at
her, oh she's grown.

She might be unsettling to look at
but that's more likely the lighting.

Cuddling her makes you realise
she isn't really that frightening.

Now, Isabella let's
discuss her too,

Izzy for short,
no matter the view.

Curiosity fills her
each passing day,

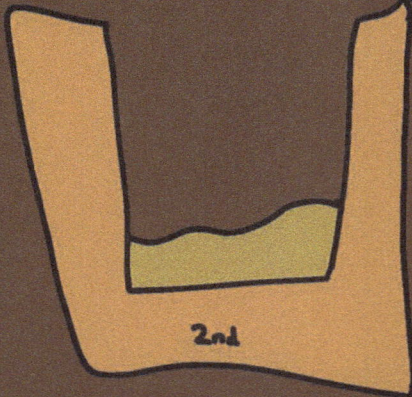

Seems like she's controlling the fray.

Ants and other things,
she enjoys her feast,

Chicken food?
Nah, it's not
her beast.

21

A black Rhode Island Plymouth Rock mix, she be,

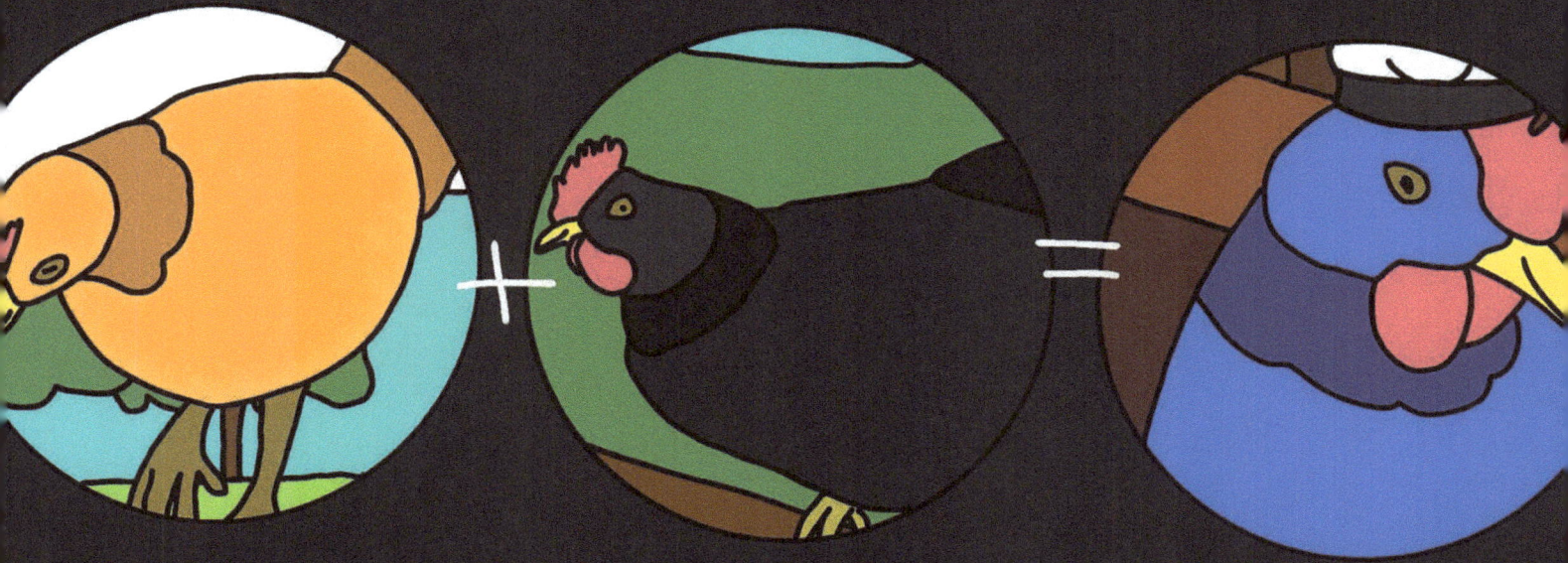

Everyone's favourite, thanks to her hybrid spree.

She likes to dash around the coop,

Running around in a loop.

Oh, how she clucks
and tweets,

Even the neighbours
can hear her feat.

She's fit to survive
fast and smart,

Loving life,
playing her part.

These are my cherished
pets, my delight,

Amazing chickens, not fully
grown, yet shining bright.

www.ingramcontent.com/pod-product-compliance
Lightning Source LLC
Chambersburg PA
CBHW041636040426

42448CB00023B/3496